God's
Power
In
Your
Life

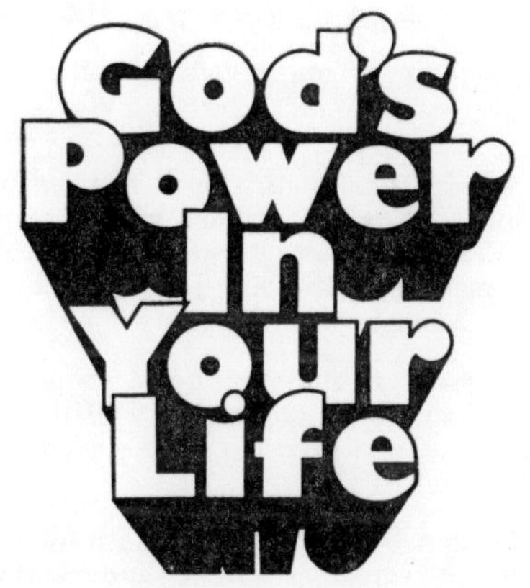

Dramas and Meditations for Lent and Easter

•

Barbara Hudson Dudley
and Richard Z. Meyer

AUGSBURG PUBLISHING HOUSE
Minneapolis, Minnesota

GOD'S POWER IN YOUR LIFE

Contents

Preface 7

Drama Production Notes 9

With God's Power in Your Life You Can:

1. Be Spontaneous in Christian Action
Mark 14:1-16 11
    Order of Worship—11
    Drama—14
    Meditation—23

2. Enjoy Your Bread with Others
Mark 14:17-31 27
    Order of Worship—27
    Drama—30
    Meditation—37

3. Pray with the Assurance of Victory
Mark 14:32-52 41
    Order of Worship—41
    Drama—44
    Meditation—52

4. Feel Good Because God Has Forgiven You
Mark 14:53-72 56
    Order of Worship—56
    Drama—59
    Meditation—67

5. Face Life with Courage
Mark 15:1-15 71
    Order of Worship—71
    Drama—74
    Meditation—81

6. Live Life with Love
Mark 15:21-39 85
    Order of Worship—85
    Drama—88
    Meditation—97

7. Live a Joyful Life
Mark 16:1-8 101
    Drama—101
    Meditation—108

Preface

God's Power in Your Life is a series of chancel dramas and meditations to help Christians receive more joy in practicing their Christian faith. The Good News of the crucified-risen Lord is the stimulus for Christians to live more abundant and fulfilled lives.

The Gospel according to Mark is the basis for the readings and the texts. We suggest that arrangements be made for every member to receive his or her own personal copy of Mark. Check with the American Bible Society for inexpensive copies of Mark, either in the Revised Standard Version or the Today's English Version. These individual copies can be used during the worship service as well as for personal reading at home.

To use this book for greatest advantage we offer the following comments:

• Chancel dramas are not just plays or skits. They are a dramatic way of putting across a message in a meaningful and helpful manner. To use this medium effectively, check the "Production Notes" carefully.

• The meditations go hand in hand with the chancel dramas. The pastor should be well acquainted with the dramas so he can use the meditations effectively. The impression should not be given that two things are happening—a meditation plus a drama—but that both are a unity in presenting the Word of God.

• The Orders of Worship are guides for use in preparing the service. The worship leaders will want to choose hymns and special music to fit both theme and people.

• The "card-of-the-week" is a way to let the people take the message home and put it into practice during the week. This may be a way of incorporating the people's responses and witness in the worship services. One way is to collect them and share the contents for all to hear. Such sharing involves the people and reenforces the message to add a lively dimension to worship.

Congregations may duplicate copy for Orders of Worship and card-of-the-week without requesting permission from the publisher.

We pray that through these dramas and meditations the life of our Lord may renew the faith and life of Christians everywhere.

BARBARA HUDSON DUDLEY
RICHARD Z. MEYER

Drama Production Notes

These plays are planned as a series of seven plays for Lent and Easter, but they may be used any time of the year, in a series or singly. There are four characters, two men and two women, in each of the plays. Any combination may be used. The same four people can do all seven plays or twenty-eight different people may be used.

A great way to use the plays in your community would be to start early and get six different churches involved. Have each church prepare one play. Then during the six weeks of Lent, each group will tour to each of the other five churches. A second group from each church (or the touring group) will do the Easter play in their own church on Easter morning so all will be able to worship in their own church on Easter. In this way six churches have seven different plays presented yet each church only has to prepare two plays.

The play scripts may be put in identical folders and read with the actors sitting on stools, or part read and part acted out. Ideally the entire play will be memorized. Even if the scripts are used, the more preparation, rehearsal, and memorization used, the more effective the production.

Simple props are necessary in only two plays, and simple costumes in one play. While no costumes as such are needed, it will be more effective if there is a uniformity of appearance: everyone in slacks and sweaters, or the women in long skirts and matching tops, or whatever you desire.

Settings: none are necessary. The plays are written for presentation in the chancel. You may use four stools, benches, the steps, or simple backdrops.

Move naturally and freely to get variety in action: at least change stools! As you rehearse, ideas will come to you for action. The more you rehearse, the more ideas, the better the performance. Make the best preparation you can, and *then* ask the Lord's blessing upon you.

BARBARA HUDSON DUDLEY

1

Be Spontaneous in Christian Action

Order of Worship

The Prelude

The Hymn:

The Responsive Reading from Romans 8 (TEV)

P. There is no condemnation now for those who live in union with Christ Jesus. For the law of the Spirit which brings us life in union with Christ Jesus, has set me free from the law of sin and death

C. This is Good News, Lord. Thank you!

P. Those who live as their human nature tells them to, have their minds controlled by what human nature wants. Those who live as the Spirit tells them to, have their minds controlled by what the Spirit wants.

C. Fill us with your Spirit, Lord!

P. If the Spirit of God, who raised Jesus from
    death, lives in you, then he who raised Christ
    from death will also give life to your mortal
    bodies by the presence of his Spirit in you.
    God's Spirit joins himself to our spirits to de-
    clare that we are God's children.

C. Spirit of God, help us now to live as God's
    children.

P. Since we are his children, we will possess the
    blessings he keeps for his people, and we will
    also possess with Christ what God has kept for
    him; for if we share Christ's suffering, we will
    also share his glory.

C. We want to follow you, Lord, on your way of
    suffering so that we may also share in your
    glory.

The Scripture: Mark 14:1-16

The Chancel Drama and Meditation

The Hymn:

The Offering of Gifts

The Distribution of the Card-of-the-Week

The Prayers

The Hymn:

The Benediction

(Copy for Card-of-the-week)

MY SPONTANEITY PRAYER

Lord, my God, remind me this week that "spontaneity" is a characteristic of your Spirit moving with my spirit. Let this kind of spontaneity loose in my life, and if possible, let me see the blessings such a word or action of love may bring. In the name of my Savior. Amen.

Readings for the Week: Mark 14:1-16 and Romans 8.

Use the back of this card to share one thing you felt you did spontaneously "in the Spirit" this week.

Be Spontaneous in Christian Action

CHARACTERS:

BEN

CATHY

LARRY

BARBARA

PROPS:

Pitcher

White "alabaster" box

COSTUMES:

Four robes or shawls to be donned over regular costumes to give suggestion of biblical character.

BEN: You can't win! All my life I've tried not to be impulsive. My dad always told me, "Stop, think, weigh the consequences. If you're impulsive, you'll get into trouble!"

CATHY: I've heard those words many times.

BEN: On my report cards the teachers used to write, "You are too impulsive. You must learn more self-control." Now, *you* say, "Be impulsive!"

BARBARA: If we're *Christ*-controlled instead of *self*-controlled, we can do things impulsively in *his* will.

LARRY: There *are* impulses that we *shouldn't* give way to.

BARBARA: True. For instance, I'm an impulsive shopper. I buy things I don't need or that are too expensive.

BEN: I blurt out my angry feelings. I need to keep my temper controlled and not hurt others the way I do.

CATHY: I often write letters when I'm angry. I write things I shouldn't. It seems the letters I shouldn't write, I write, and the letters I should write, I don't!

LARRY: St. Paul's complaint.

CATHY: But let's talk about the impulses we *should* follow.

LARRY: Well, if the house is on fire, I'll impulsively yell for the fire department.

BARBARA: If my children are in danger, I'll do what I can to protect them.

BEN: If I start to fall I'll grab for support.

BARBARA: When I meet people I love, I kiss them.

LARRY: These impulses aren't the problem. The problem is when we have an impulse to do the right thing and don't do it!

CATHY: All my life I've had impulses to do good things, things I knew I should do. And then I procrastinate, and they never get done...telephone calls I should have made . . . letters I should have written...I have too much *self*-control instead of letting the Holy Spirit have control.

LARRY: I guess when we have a *good* impulse, we should do it *now* without delay.

CATHY: I know, let's act some of them out ... I'm in my kitchen—putting things away. I see the telephone and think—Mary looked so unhappy this morning—I'll call her and see if there's anything I can do for her—Oh, I guess I won't call now, I've got to fix dinner. I'll call later. I'll call her tomorrow—or maybe next week.

LARRY: And so you don't get around to calling her at all! *(pause)* I'm at a business meeting. I've just heard a great speaker. I'll go up and tell him how much it meant to me. Oh, there's such a crowd, guess I won't bother. He knows how good he is! He doesn't need me to tell him. I'm in a hurry to get home....So, I don't tell him. No one tells him!

BARBARA: That speaker *could* be the pastor on Sunday morning! ... My husband and I had a quarrel last night. The whole evening was ruined. Now, I'm getting breakfast. I'm going to tell Tom I'm sorry that the evening was spoiled. I'm going to tell him how much I appreciate him and love him!—Of course he *did* say those terrible things.

He didn't have to be so cruel. Maybe I was wrong, but *he* was wrong, too! Now that I think of it, he was more wrong than I was! I'll let *him* apologize first. *(bumps leg against a chair)*...ouch! Oh, what a terrible morning!

BEN: I ride my son pretty hard most of the time giving him advice, criticizing him. Yet I'm proud of him. He's really doing a great job. Guess I ought to tell him so...but he knows how I feel. I wouldn't say it right anyway. We speak different languages. He'd probably think I was square—or whatever word they use now. Or I'd embarrass him. I'll let it go for now. There's plenty of time.

CATHY: But maybe he doesn't know. And perhaps there isn't plenty of time.... My little girl just asked me to come outdoors to look at the flowers. "Some other time. Mother's too busy! I can't take time to look at flowers this morning. And neither should you! You ought to be in here helping me instead of looking at flowers! Don't track dirt over mother's clean floor!"

LARRY: I'm at work. The fellow at the next desk is a heavy drinker. He has lots of problems at home and troubles at work. I wish there was something I could do to help him. He really needs help. I ought to invite him to church. But he probably doesn't want to come to church. I suppose I ought to witness. But I'm not good at that sort of thing. I don't want to butt into his affairs. Maybe *next* week I'll mention church to him. Got to get that report done!

BARBARA: Anne looks lovely this afternoon. She's a

wonderful person and she's doing a great job. I ought to tell her. But then she might think I was trying to flatter her. I don't want to seem like I'm gushing. I guess I won't bother her.

BEN: Mother's getting old. I ought to write her a letter, tell her how much she's meant to me. Oh, well . . . she knows it without my telling her. Besides it's time for the game on TV. I'll do it next week.

CATHY: *Do we ever do anything right?*

LARRY: We're cowards!

BARBARA: We've all got lots of impulses we can start acting on.

BEN: Like the two we read about in the Scriptures.

BARBARA: Those wonderful, impulsive people who did the right thing, Mary with her perfume, and the man with the water jug on his head.

BEN: I wonder how they felt? What was going on in their minds?

CATHY: Let's act it out.

BEN: You be Mary and you two be the disciples. I'll be Jesus!
(*All put on robes or shawls.*)

CATHY: It's a beautiful spring evening. I'm carrying a white alabaster box filled with ointment. This is the garden outside the house where Jesus is meeting with the disciples. I feel so much love for Jesus, such gratitude that I have this impulse to anoint his feet. But I mustn't go in. A woman should never go into a gathering of men! It was foolish to take all my money and buy ointment. I'll be a nuisance and people will laugh at me. I'll make a fool of myself. . . . I don't care. I will go in! I don't care what they say. I will kneel at Jesus' feet before them all and show my love for him!

LARRY: Where are you going? You can't come in here. No women allowed!

CATHY: Please let me in. I must see Jesus.

LARRY: You shouldn't be in here! This is no place for a woman!

BARBARA: What's she doing? Has she no shame!

LARRY: Doesn't she know her place? Look at her? She's breaking the alabaster box and pouring perfume on Jesus' feet.

BARBARA: That's expensive!

LARRY: What a waste!

BARBARA: Why, the money should have been given to the poor. What does she think she's doing anyway! Get her out of there!

BEN: (*As Jesus, turns towards others.*) Leave her alone. She is doing it out of love. The poor you will always have with you. Remember them when I am no longer with you. She has prepared me for my burial.

LARRY: Don't talk like that! You aren't going to die. You're going to lead us to victory!

BEN: The day is soon coming when I will no longer

be with you. When I am gone, and whenever men talk of me, let them also tell about Mary and what she has done this night.

CATHY: Why, he's pleased with what I did. And I almost didn't have the courage to do it. But I did it. And he's pleased!

BEN: You were very brave, Mary, and because you didn't think of yourself, you will be remembered forever.

CATHY: *(Removing shawl.)* End of scene! Now I'm me! I hope I can be impulsive as Mary was and do those things that will bring happiness to others. If I feel it's the right thing, I'll do it! Now, Larry, you do the story about the man carrying the pitcher of water. We'll call you Jason.

LARRY: *(Picks up large pitcher.)* Okay, I'll be Jason. You be my wife. You have a fever and you're very ill. Your name is Miriam.

BARBARA: All right.

LARRY: How are you feeling, Miriam?

BARBARA: I'm so hot and thirsty.

LARRY: I'll get you some water.

BARBARA: You can't do that! They'll say you have a lazy wife if you have to go to the well for water. Only women go to the well—you know that! They'll laugh at you. They can be so unkind.

LARRY: So let them laugh! Do you think that will hurt me? What hurts is to see you lying there with fever and no water to bathe your face or give you a cool drink. Rest while I get the water. I'll hurry ... everyone is looking at me but I don't care. The important thing is to get the water ... there are some men pointing at me. Let them point! Maybe they should go home and help their wives! Am I doing something criminal by carrying a pitcher of water? ... Why are you following me? Have you never seen a pitcher before? Have you never seen a *man* before?

BEN: Forgive us, friend. But we were told by the master to find a man carrying a pitcher of water.

LARRY: What for? What have I done? My wife is sick and she needs water. Leave me alone. Who's your master, anyway?

BEN: Jesus, the Messiah!

LARRY: The Messiah! *He* told you to follow *me?*

BEN: He told us to find a man carrying a pitcher of water and follow him to his home and there prepare the Passover feast.

LARRY: And I am that man! To think that Jesus is coming to my house for Passover! Silly women, laugh at me all you want. What do I care? Jesus will dine in my house tonight! *(Puts down pitcher.)* End of scene! Hey, I felt like I was right there. *(Takes off robe.)*

BEN: *(Takes off robe.)* You really get into it when you try to put yourself in the other person's place.

BARBARA: *(Taking off robe.)* It's thrilling to do things impulsively for Christ.

LARRY: Witness ...

CATHY: Write letters of love ...

BEN: Telephone ...

BARBARA: Apologize ...

LARRY: Say the right word at the right time.

CATHY: Dear Lord, take my hands and let them move at the *impulse of thy love.*

LARRY: Take my voice and let me sing always, only, for my King.

BARBARA: Take my feet and let them be swift and beautiful for thee.

BEN: Take my moments and my days, let them flow in ceaseless praise.

CATHY: Take my life and let it be consecrated, Lord, to thee.

ALL: Amen.

Be Spontaneous in Christian Action

Mark 14:1-16

There is something about Mary and the man with the jug of water that is enviable. Their spontaneous actions reveal the kind of love that we like to see in Christians. What is more important, we like to see it in ourselves.

Some actions need careful thought. We need to calculate certain decisions carefully before we act. When we buy a house, for example, we would hardly make such a large purchase without carefully analyzing the financing, surveying the neighborhood, and investigating the schools. It is a decision that requires more calculated reasoning than reacting on a spontaneous impulse.

Spontaneous actions can also reveal the impulsive spirit of our sinful and rebellious nature. When we hit back rather than turn the other cheek, or when we curse someone out instead of speaking the kind and loving word, we express a type of spontaneity Jesus described when he said "Out of the heart come evil thoughts, murder, adultery, fornication, theft, false witness, slander" (Matthew 15:19). So just to be spontaneous and impulsive is not necessarily a virtue.

What makes Mary and the man in our chancel drama so attractive is not just their actions of love, but the kind of heart their actions reveal. It is the changed heart that gives wholesome and loving expression to spontaneous actions. St. Augustine told a young man who asked what should he do and not do: "Love God with all your heart and do as you please." When the heart is filled with the love of God, we do not have to be afraid of our actions. This does not rule out our mind; rather it frees up our mind and our heart to respond to the needs of others in the joy of the Spirit.

Our Lenten pilgrimage will help us see that God's power revealed in the life of Jesus Christ is for each of us. This evening we see that with Jesus we can be spontaneous in our Christian actions. In our reading from St. Mark, we see Mary perform a spontaneous act of service.

Mary does a strange and wonderful thing to honor the Master whom she loves so deeply. She anoints his feet with a very expensive ointment, an anointing Jesus interprets as an anointing for his burial. It was the custom of that time to anoint the body with nard and then to break the container. This Mary does in a quiet, reverent, moving scene before all the other guests. In spite of their criticism and negative remarks she does what she feels she must do. Thank God she did! Jesus was certainly grateful. He said, "Wherever the Good News shall be proclaimed throughout the whole world, the story of what she has done will be told, so that she will always be remembered."

You may think, "That was very thoughtful of Jesus." Not just thoughtful! Jesus said that Mary's act would be remembered because her action was a clear manifestation of the Gospel, a loving expression of what God was doing for the whole world. That is why Jesus said what he did.

Mary's spontaneous expression of love is a marvelous example for us. Love always has a certain extravagance to it. We give an expensive gift to someone we love, and the beloved with surprise and delight responds, "Oh, you should not have done it!" Love never counts the cost. In Mary we see no calculated love, that "how much will it cost" kind of thinking. There is a recklessness in Mary's act that is refreshing. She just did what she felt no matter what. And through her action she proclaimed the Gospel.

This kind of love can recognize the once-in-a-lifetime opportunities. It is one of the tragedies of life that we often let these opportunities slip by. We give them too many second thoughts. We become afraid of what others might say. We conclude that we might be considered stupid and foolish. We rationalize that it might not be so important after all. The tragedy is that too many impulses are strangled at birth. This would be a lovelier world if more of us would be able to act like Mary, letting the spontaneity that comes in the Gospel show through to others.

If you want this kind of spontaneity and if you desire the kind of love that can act without always counting the cost, then look not at Mary, but to Jesus. For it was from Jesus that the love was born for the holy impulse to do what she did.

Even at this moment in the passion history we can

see the invincible confidence of Jesus to fulfill the strange plan of God for the world's redemption. In Jesus we see the strange, divine impulse that revealed a reckless abandoning of counting the cost and plunging into the heart of all evil, sin, and death, so that those ensnarled could be rescued. Nothing reveals the heart of God more fully than the cross. Here is the unconditional, non-calculating, self-giving love that becomes the redemptive power to change the hearts and lives of people. It is out of this divine love that all divine impulses can flow in the world. Look at Mary!

Do you want to become more spontaneous in your Christian actions and express more naturally the new life of the Spirit of God? Then open up again to the unconditional love of God that he has poured out abundantly in his Son. The Good News is that this divine love can and will fill your hearts and minds, so that you can feel how natural it is to respond spontaneously to the movement of the Spirit. Then you will feel free to say that "thank you," or to give that friend the good word, or to say that apology, or to visit that certain person, or to do that little "extra" for someone who is so dear to you. Believe it! With Jesus you can be spontaneous in Christian action.

2

Enjoy Your Bread with Others

Order of Worship

The Prelude

The Hymn:

The Responsive Reading from Ezekiel 34 and John 10

P. Thus says the Lord God: Ho, shepherds of Israel who have been feeding yourselves! Should not shepherds feed the sheep? The weak you have not strengthened, the sick you have not healed, the crippled you have not bound up, the strayed you have not brought back, the lost you have not sought.

C. Forgive us, O Lord our God, for the times we have not fed and helped each other as we ought.

P. Thus says the Lord God: "Behold, I, I myself will search for my sheep, and will seek them out . . . I will rescue them . . . I will feed them . . . I myself will be the shepherd of my sheep

...I will seek the lost...bring back the strayed ... bind up the crippled ... and I will feed them in justice."

C. We give you thanks, O Lord our God, for being our shepherd, seeking us out and feeding us all that we need.

P. Thus says the Lord God: "I will set up over them one shepherd, my servant David, and he shall feed them; he shall feed them and be their shepherd.

C. This we know and believe, and this is why we are here. For we know the shepherd and he knows us. And he told us, "I am the Good Shepherd, and the Good Shepherd lays down his life for the sheep."

P. The Good Shepherd said: "I have other sheep that are not of this fold; I must bring them also, and they will heed my voice."

C. "So there shall be one flock, one shepherd." Praise be to you, O Christ!

The Lesson: Mark 14:17-31

The Hymn:

The Drama and Meditation

The Song:

Let us break bread together on our knees.
Let us break bread together on our knees.
When I fall on my knees with my face to the
rising sun,
O Lord, have mercy on me.
Let us drink wine together on our knees ...
Let us praise God together on our knees ...

The Offering of Gifts

The Distribution of the Card-of-the-Week

The Prayers

The Hymn:

The Benediction

(Copy for Card-of-the-Week)

MY PRAYER FOR THE FAMILY OF BELIEVERS

Lord, I know that the fellowship of my Christian brothers and sisters is a sign of your unfailing grace. Let me enjoy this family of believers by breaking bread with them, so that together we may be edified in faith and love. In the name of our Savior who creates the new community. Amen

Readings for the Week: Mark 14:17-31, Ezekiel 34.

This week try to invite another family or person to eat with you, and jot down the blessing in this act of fellowship.

Enjoy Your Bread with Others

CHARACTERS:

Lois

Jean

Dan

Matt

PROPS:

Picnic basket

Food

Dan: Spread the embers of the fire about and the fire goes out.

Jean: Isolate the members of a church from Christian fellowship and the *spiritual* fire goes out.

Matt: But just sitting together in church for an hour on Sunday morning doesn't get much fire going!

Lois: The warmest Christians are those who spend many hours together in many activities.

DAN: And breaking bread together is one of the best ways to fellowship.

MATT: Well, I don't think that eating together is the same thing as a church service!

JEAN: Look how many times Jesus ate with his disciples!

LOIS: Yes, and he used those times for teaching his most important lessons!

DAN: He preached to the multitudes as they munched on the loaves and fishes he multiplied.

JEAN: I can see him sitting on the shore of the Sea of Galilee by a campfire, broiling a fish...

MATT: The disciples laughing...

LOIS: And joking, sharing food...

DAN: And talking...

JEAN: As the moonlight made silver patterns on the dark blue water.

MATT: Very poetic! That's a nice idea.

LOIS: When you think about it, it seems they were *always* eating!

DAN: Fish and honey...

JEAN: Fruit...

MATT: And fresh baked bread.

DAN: He ate with Mary and Martha.

JEAN: He ate at the wedding feast at Cana.

MATT: The funeral feast turned into a festival of praise at Lazarus' tomb.

LOIS: And there was the supper with the tree-climber Zacchaeus.

DAN: He ate with Matthew, the tax collector who became his disciple.

JEAN: He went to the home of one of the Pharisees and ate bread on the Sabbath day.

MATT: They ate at the last supper.

LOIS: Even after the resurrection Jesus came back and ate with the disciples.

DAN: The great thing is that Jesus didn't care whether he ate with rich or poor, publican or Pharisees.

JEAN: And along with the food, Christ offers us the bread of *life.* He offers the banquet of love without price.

MATT: Come, without money and without price and buy milk and honey.

LOIS: Jesus said, "Everyone who thirsts, drink of the living water that I shall give you and you shall never thirst again."

DAN: We should eat together in Christian fellowship more often.

JEAN: How about now? *(Brings out picnic basket.)* I brought enough for all. *(Opens basket and passes food to the other three. They sit down for a picnic.)*

MATT: When you go to a man's house and sit at his table you really feel that you know him and are welcome in his life.

LOIS: Invite a stranger to your table and he becomes your friend.

DAN: And while you are eating it's a wonderful time to witness for Christ for when a man eats with you, he is much more receptive to your ideas.

JEAN: Isn't there a saying that if you have shared food with a man at his table you must never betray him?

LOIS: The one who broke that rule was Judas.

MATT: And you know what happened to him.

JEAN: Here. Try some of this. *(Hands him a piece of bread.)*

DAN: Thank you.

MATT: One good thing about eating together is that you have to listen. You can't talk all the time! And when the disciples ate with Jesus, I'm sure they did most of the listening!

DAN: *(Refers to food.)* This is good!

LOIS: I remember when my children were small, they were always so demanding at meal times— in a nice sort of way! They would spill things— and have to go to the bathroom! I used to wish I could eat in a beautiful restaurant without them so they couldn't bother me. Well, I had to leave them for three weeks one time and I had my fill of beautiful restaurants without them. I got so lonely for them I would have given *anything* to have them there asking to go to the bathroom! I couldn't wait to get home.

MATT: I guess the Lord wants us to use meal times for fellowship. We constantly need to eat. Every day all over again we need to eat the same amount of food no matter what happens.

JEAN: This is wonderful. A banquet with Christ and fellow believers. What a glorious party!

DAN: I don't think we are to limit our fellowship to fellow believers. Sharing a meal with an unbeliever is a good way to share the fellowship of Christ with him.

MATT: That's right. Christ gave us instructions about that in Luke 14. "When you have a dinner or supper, do not invite your friends nor your brother, nor your relatives, nor your rich neighbors lest they return the invitation to you and you are paid back for your hospitality."

JEAN: "But when you make a feast, call the poor, the maimed, the lame and the blind and you will be blessed, for they cannot recompense you, but you will be recompensed at the resurrection of the just."

LOIS: I would like to invite people to my house but I don't fix very fancy meals . . . just plain food.

DAN: Christ said that if we offer a cup of cold water in his name we will be blessed.

MATT: Well, I guess I could supply that much!

JEAN: The fellowship is the important thing to share. If we share what we have, Christ will bless.

LOIS: My home isn't very fancy. Does anyone want to come there?

DAN: However plain it is, if Christ's love is there it will be a castle and a refuge to the lonely.

JEAN: This all reminds me of a poem I wrote once. Want to hear it?

MATT: Sure! Go ahead!

JEAN: Poets write such lovely things, artists paint such beauty, singers soar away on wings, doctors do their duty. There is nothing I can do, that's quite plain to see! Yet I make good Irish stew, so please, come dine with me!

DAN: Hey, that's all right!

JEAN: I invite you all to my house for dinner to-morrow.

MATT: And a stranger! Let's each invite a stranger!

LOIS: What a pleasant prospect . . . sharing food, talking, laughing . . .

JEAN: What a wonderful life to be in the family of God.

DAN: Blessed is he that shall eat bread in the king-dom of heaven.

MATT: Come to my house, to my house come.

LOIS: We'll have food, fellowship, and fun!

DAN: You're all poets! Let's have a church dinner soon so we can all break bread together.

JEAN: The communion service should be a happy time, a time of joy and thanksgiving and remem-brance of Christ.

MATT: What kind of menu can we get from the Scriptures?

LOIS: There's milk.

DAN: Honey.

JEAN: Fish.

MATT: Wine!

LOIS: Bread.

DAN: And the fruits of the spirit!

JEAN: Love—

MATT: Joy—

LOIS: Peace—

DAN: Long suffering—

JEAN: Patience—

MATT: Hope—!

DAN: During the week, let's invite someone to dinner in our home for Christian fellowship, food and fun.

(Actors get up and go through congregation passing food out to worshipers as they sing, "We will break bread together.")

Enjoy Your Bread with Others

Mark 14:17-31

Daily bread and Christian fellowship are two things we often take for granted. They are here today, and we have no worry that they will be here tomorrow. Even with rising prices, our tables have been laden with food this week, and we are not fearful that they won't be so laden in the weeks to come. We are gathered together as a community of believing men and women this evening. We have no worry that this community of Christians will be here next month. Like the rising and the setting of the sun, we assume we will always have daily bread and Christian fellowship.

Yet the fact remains that it is by the sheer grace of God that we are allowed to live in fellowship with Christian brothers and sisters. Our fellowship with each other is a gift of grace. It has come from God, and it can be taken by God. It is a sign of God's love and mercy that we gather here together this evening. It is a sign of his presence in the midst of a world that refuses to let him be God.

It is also by the sheer grace of God that we have daily bread. The bread passed out this evening by the actors in our chancel drama is evidence of the providential care of the Almighty. Non-believers would scoff at such an assertion. They believe that daily bread is explained by some economic principle. But we still pray, "Give us this day our daily bread," because we believe that daily bread is a gift from God for which we give him thanks. Faith opens our eyes to see daily bread as a sign of God's goodness in our world.

Jesus certainly looked at daily bread and the fellowship of believers as a sign of his heavenly Father's blessing in his own life. That is one reason why Jesus wanted to have supper with his disciples in the upper room. He wanted to celebrate the Passover with them, for the Passover was the commemoration of the redemptive act of God for his people. Jesus wanted very much the disciples' friendship in these hours of growing anxiety. He knew the blessing of such community. And Jesus wanted to have this supper with his disciples because he knew that they needed this communal meal with him. During this "Last Supper" the disciples certainly did not grasp all that it meant that night, but they never forgot it. At this supper the Lord instituted a very special meal that would draw all Christians to Jesus and to each other. At this meal his followers would discover again and again the meaning of being forgiven, and the purpose of being together.

The Scripture indicates three kinds of table fellowship that Jesus keeps with his own: daily fellowship at the meal table; the table fellowship of the Lord's Supper; and the final table fellowship in the kingdom of God. And in all three one thing always happens:

whenever the bread is blessed and shared, to use the words of St. Luke, "their eyes were opened, and they knew him!" (Luke 24:30-31). To know Jesus in the presence of these gifts shared with other believers is a reassuring experience.

When we pray, "Come, Lord Jesus, be our guest . . .," we believe that Christ is present with us. Every mealtime fills us with gratitude not only for the food set before us but for the living, present Lord. Therefore, we are bound together not only by the common food we share, but by him who is the honored guest at the table. Our eyes of faith are open, and we know Jesus.

It means that the meal table has a festive quality. It is a reminder that in the midst of all our labors, there is a time for refreshment and joy in the goodness of God. As Ecclesiastes exhorts: "Eat thy bread with joy (9:7); and again, "I commend enjoyment, because a man has no good thing under the sun but to eat, and drink, and enjoy himself" (8:15); but the holy writer also says, "apart from him (the Lord) who can eat or who can have enjoyment?" (2:25). Through our daily meals our Lord calls us to rejoice in his mercy, to keep the holiday, right in the midst of our working day.

We begin to see that the right way of eating and drinking prepares us for the proper reception of Holy Communion. All mealtimes prepare us for the Holy Communion, and all Communions prepare us for the feast in Paradise. That is why for Christians ordinary mealtimes can be extraordinary times!

It is not accidental, therefore, that on the way to the cross our Lord takes time to sit down and have a very special meal with his disciples. In fact he uses this meal as a means to bless all the other mealtimes of believers. He takes bread and wine, and communicates to his church his body and blood, uniting it with his redemption and sealing it in his destiny.

It is good that we can enjoy each other. It is good for us to eat together. Did you hear the last words in the drama? "During the week, let's invite someone to dinner in our home." Why not? Enjoy the fellowship Christ has given us! Enjoy the gifts of daily bread, all signs of his grace and love. Let your mealtimes take on special meaning, whether you serve hot dogs or steak. What matters is that you can see what God is doing as you share bread in the name of Jesus Christ. Yes, with Jesus you can enjoy your bread with others . . . every day!

3

Pray with the Assurance of Victory

Order of Worship

The Prelude

The Hymn:

The Responsive Reading from Psalm 22 (TEV)

P. My God, my God, why have you abandoned me? I have cried desperately for help, but it still does not come! During the day I call to you, my God, but you do not answer; I call at night, but get no rest.

C. Lord Jesus, that you experienced the depths of my human condition so fully as to cry out to the Father like this simply overwhelms me. I, too, have felt this struggle of faith.

P. But I am no longer a man; I am a worm, despised and scorned by all! All who see me make fun of me; they stick out their tongues and shake their heads. "You relied on the Lord,"

41

they say. "Why doesn't he save you? If the Lord likes you, why doesn't he help you?"

C. Lord Jesus, my Savior, how you were tempted in the last hours of your passion! To drink the cup given by the Father was not easy. Thank you, Lord, for doing the Father's will.

P. A gang of evil men is around me; like a pack of dogs, they close in on me; they pierce my hands and my feet. All my bones can be seen. My enemies look at me and stare; they divide my clothes among themselves and gamble for my robe.

C. Lord Jesus, my Savior, how clearly I see the picture of your cross! And because you have suffered and been tempted in all things common to all men, you are able to help me in anything.

P. All nations will remember the Lord; from every part of the world they will turn to him; all races will worship him. The Lord is king, and he rules over the nations.

C. Lord Jesus, my Savior, I join with those who worship you as "Lord of the nations." Regardless of my personal struggles and inadequacies, I will serve you whatever the cost. Praise be to you, O Christ!

The Lesson: Mark 14:32-52

The hymn:

The Drama and Meditation

The Song: Sweet hour of prayer, sweet hour of prayer, That calls me from a world of care, And bids me at my Father's throne Make all my wants and wishes known. In seasons of distress and grief, My soul has often found relief, And oft escaped the tempter's snare, by thy return, sweet hour of prayer.

The Offering of Our Gifts

The Distribution of the Card-of-the-Week

The Prayers

The Hymn:

The Benediction

(Copy for Card-of-the-Week)

MY PRAYER FOR ASSURANCE

Lord, I struggle with many things. How I want your help. Teach me to pray my will into your own. And being part of your will, let me taste the blessings you give in answering my prayer. Amen.

Readings: Mark 14:32-52 and Psalm 22

This week take special time in prayer, preferably with someone else, to pray through some of the burdens with which you struggle. Share this burden on the back of the card, and if possible, the answer God has given you.

Pray with the Assurance of Victory

CHARACTERS:

PETE

JIM

KATE

TERI

PETE: How wonderful it is—

KATE: To have the opportunity to pray—

JIM: To have faith that our prayers are heard instantly—

TERI: At the throne of grace.

PETE: With Christ our Savior as our righteousness, our advocate—

KATE: And the Holy Spirit as our intercessor—

JIM: We can bring to God our prayers of praise—

TERI: Love—

PETE: Loneliness—

KATE: Sorrow—

JIM: Joy—

TERI: Defeat—

PETE: Petition—

KATE: Intercession—

TERI: Thanksgiving—

JIM: And silence.

KATE: Let's sing together—

TERI: Meaningfully—

JIM: Prayerfully—

PETE: The hymn "Sweet Hour of Prayer."

(Congregation and actors sing hymn.)

> Sweet hour of prayer, sweet hour of prayer
> That calls me from a world of care
> And bids me at my father's throne
> Make all my wants and wishes known.
> In seasons of distress and grief
> My soul has often found relief
> And oft escaped the tempter's snare
> By thy return sweet hour of prayer.

(After hymn, the four actors sit on altar steps.)

KATE: We sing and talk so much about prayer, but how are we supposed to pray?

JIM: So much of prayer is just wild, desperate phrases throw nout into a void at the time of crisis and emergency.

TERI: We are to pray without ceasing like breathing out and breathing in—a constant conversation with God.

PETE: We can create a symphony of prayer with seven steps.

KATE: A seven step symphony of prayer! Very good! First step—

JIM: Start your prayer with *praise* for our Heavenly Father — praise, worship, adoration, reverence. The second step—

TERI: *Thanksgiving* for our blessings, for all good things great and small, known and unknown. Third step—

PETE: Confession of all known sins of commission and omission, and repentance of our sins, known and unknown. Fourth step—

KATE: *Intercession*—for all those who have asked for our prayers and for all those who need our prayers though they may not have asked for them. Fifth step—

JIM: *Petition*—making our requests known unto God. Asking the Holy Spirit to intercede for us and to request those things that he knows we need. Sixth step—

TERI: *Thanksgiving* for the answers we know that we will receive. Seventh step—

JIM: End it all with *praise* again and we have finished the seven steps in our symphony of prayer. Praise, thanksgiving, confession, intercession, petition, thanksgiving and praise.

KATE: Does it matter what words we use when we pray?

PETE: No! Let them tumble out. God listens to our hearts—not our sentence structure.

TERI: You mean I don't have to worry about using *thee, thou, hast,* and *thine?*

JIM: No. say it in your own way. The Holy Spirit will translate for us and put our prayers into language too beautiful for us to imagine.

KATE: What is the answer that will keep you from sinning? Pray for that answer. Be specific. But don't limit God to *your* viewpoint! He knows far better than we do what's best for us.

PETE: It's common to pray, "Lord, *use* me." But what if the Lord doesn't want to use me? Are we willing to pray, "Lord, *don't* use me if that is your will? Set me aside. Let me wander in the wilderness, *if that is your will.*"

TERI: It's common to pray, "Lord, use me to do *big* things, great things!!" Are we just as willing to pray that the Lord will use us in small ways, small things, to do the little jobs that need to be done? Nothing is small in God's sight . . . only in ours. Too many of us want to do the things that will bring fame and glory, and we forget to seek out the small task, right at hand, that needs doing.

PETE: It's common to pray for success. We must be willing to *fail* if that will bring God the greater glory! We must forget self and selfish demands and wishes, and surrender ourselves to those things that will honor God, not ourselves. Sometimes the Lord wants us to do a big job and we're afraid to do it because we might fail but we must remember that God has promised to give us the strength that we need to do his will.

KATE: We are so involved with the *problem* that brings us to our knees in prayer that we forget to focus on the *solution* to the problem. Reach out for the solution. The answer may be right there within reach. Do not focus on the problem. Focus on the solution.

JIM: It's common to pray, "I won't! I don't want your will!" We need to be transformed by the Holy Spirit so that our "I *won't!*" becomes his *will.*

TERI: When we say "Your will be done!" to God, what peace there is, the struggle gone.

KATE: How beautiful is the peace that comes from total surrender to God.

PETE: Whether I live or die, I am the Lord's.

TERI: Whether sick or well, I am the Lord's.

JIM: Whether rich or poor, I am the Lord's.

KATE: Whether I'm used or not, I am the Lord's.

PETE: Whether married or single—

TERI: Whether man or woman—

JIM: Whether I do great works or the smallest task at hand—

KATE: Whether young or old—

ALL: We are the Lord's!

PETE: Whether black, white, yellow, brown or red—

TERI: Whether I am weak or strong—

PETE: Tall or short—

KATE: Thin or fat—

ALL: We are the Lord's!

JIM: Whether people appreciate me or not—

TERI: Whether I'm a success or a failure—

PETE: Whether I'm happy or sad—

KATE: Whether I'm praised or rejected—

ALL: We are the Lord's!

JIM: Whether I speak or am silent—

ALL: We are the Lord's!

TERI: The apostle Paul said, "I have learned, in whatever state I am in, to be content."

ALL: Thy will be done. Blessed be the name of the Lord.

KATE: God, are you really there?

PETE: Is there a presence who fills our lives?

TERI: I don't want to live a lonely life—

JIM: An empty life—

KATE: A defeated life.

PETE: God, prove to me that you are there!

TERI: No voice speaks in the silence.

KATE: And yet, I feel his presence.

TERI: I feel warm and happy.

JIM: I am smiling—

PETE: Filled with joy—

KATE: Peace—

JIM: And happiness—

TERI: That does not come from *my* empty, lonely heart.

PETE: I know it comes from God, the presence of Christ and the Holy Spirit.

KATE: God is waiting for our prayers.

JIM: Let us eagerly, joyously, confidently bow in prayer—

TERI: Knowing that Christ has promised that anything we ask in his name shall be done to the glory of God—

PETE: Knowing the Holy Spirit has promised to be our intercessor.

KATE: We remember Jesus that night in Gethsemane when he prayed to his Father—

JIM: "Not what I will, but what thou wilt."

TERI: Everyone pray it together. *(Include congregation.)*

ALL: "Not what I will, but what thou wilt."

PETE: Thank you, God, for taking away the sharp, sour, vinegar of self from our souls.

KATE: Thank you for taking away the twisted, ugly bitterness of personal pride...

JIM: The grasping, scheming ugliness of personal plans . . .

TERI: The gray, shadowy, loneliness that comes from living for self alone.

PETE: Lord, melt us, cleanse us, mould us, fill us, use us.

PETE: Fill us with your presence and power.

KATE: Fill us with the love, joy, peace and victory—

JIM: That is beyond our human understanding because it comes from you.

ALL: Amen.

Pray with the Assurance of Victory

Mark 14:32-52

"God is waiting for our prayers," one of our actors just told us in our drama. God is waiting for our prayers because he wants us to grow into the full stature of his sons and daughters, just as we who are parents wait for our child to begin talking. As the child learns to articulate his feelings and verbally respond to yours, communication becomes stronger between parent and child. Parents who know how to listen to their children help them understand themselves better and to grow up in the best possible way.

God is waiting for our prayers, too, because he wants to listen to us in such a way that we grow in our understanding of ourselves as his people, become more aware of the new, Christ-life in us, and express more clearly this life as well as our feelings, doubts, joys, and struggles.

If God is waiting for our prayers, then our prayers are important. They are important to God who wants to listen and respond. And important to us who need to grow in our understanding of our heavenly Father and of ourselves as his children. Parents and children who never talk with each other not only never grow up as a family, but actually retard each other's individual and personal growth as a human being. How many great possibilities are lost to us because we do not take time in prayer to honestly share all our feelings before God and pray ourselves more and more into his will and love for our lives.

When we see Jesus in prayer in the Garden of Gethsemane, we need to remember how natural this was for Jesus. All through his life he had been a man of prayer. He did not just pray in times of stress and trouble, but took time each day to pray to his heavenly Father. He knew the comfort and the power of prayer, so in this hour of duress and extreme inner struggle, it was a very natural thing for him to take his disciples with him to the garden so that he could have a time and a place for prayer.

Jesus prayed that night, not just out of habit, but because he knew he had to. It would be a mistake to think Jesus was play-acting here. Jesus was suffering great agony because he knew what he had to face in the coming hours. It was not just the fear of dying. Rather it was the fearsome assault of the evil one whose temptations at this hour were more frightening than those in the desert. The compelling temptation came in the thought, "Is there another way? Can I be spared the pain of suffering death to do my Father's will? Is there some way out?"

So Jesus had to pray that night. He wanted to pray himself into the will of the Father. He wanted to open up to the Father, so that the Father could open up his will to him most clearly. So Jesus prayed. And Jesus was totally refreshed. As the hours in that hideous night unfolded, we see in Jesus a very strong man, who knew what he was about as the Son of God.

If Jesus had to pray in this way to the heavenly Father, so must we. We, too, need to pray our will into the will of God. That is why we say, "Your will be done." Some just tack on, "Your will be done," to their prayers with the attitude that it makes no difference what we pray for, God will have his way in the end. Like children who ask if they can watch a late TV program on a school night, knowing mother's answer will be no, reply, "We knew you were going to say no; we don't know why we bother to ask you." And some feel this way in talking to God in prayer.

But this is not prayer. If you already know the obvious will of God, it is not something you must pray for. It is when you have difficulty with the will of God in your life, or when you need a resource outside of yourself to do what you know you must as a Christian. Then you need to pray and to pray openly and honestly, opening up to God all of your feelings and doubts and fears. Let your prayer become the soul-searching exercise that forces you to look hard at yourself. You can be confident that in your praying the Spirit of God will open up God's Word for your faith and life. He touches you with power not only to know God's will for your life more clearly, but to give you his strength to perform that will. You experience the victory that is the outcome of prayer.

Sometimes you need help in prayer. You have trouble in praying alone. You ask, "Is there a good book on prayer?" Books help. So does the support of another Christian. Jesus took with him Peter,

James, and John to be with him as he struggled in prayer. But they fell asleep, leaving Jesus very much alone. This did not help Jesus, although he understood their tired feeling. Do not be afraid to ask another Christian brother or sister to pray with you. And if you are asked, realize the privilege of praying with another. This is why many Christians have found great assistance in prayer groups. Do not feel that you have to pray alone, but do make a time and place for regular prayer.

God is waiting for our prayers. He was waiting for the prayers of his Son that night, so he could give him the needed strength to walk the way of the cross. The Father was also waiting for his Son to experience the joy and victory of that strange and myterious route for the world's redemption. He wanted Jesus to experience the victory revealed so emphatically in the resurrection. This victory of Christ over all the tyrants that hold us fast in death and hell is the Good News for each of us. God is waiting for each of us to experience more fully the joy and the power of this victory won by his Son.

God is waiting for your prayers. He wants to listen to you, to help you grow up as his child, to send his Spirit to open up his word for your faith and life, and above all, to make real the victory you have in his Son. With Jesus you can pray with the assurance of victory!

4

Feel Good Because God Has Forgiven You

Order of Worship

The Prelude

The Hymn:

The Responsive Reading from the 53rd chapter of Isaiah

> P. He grew up before him like a young plant, and like a root out of dry ground; he had no form or comeliness that we should look at him, and no beauty that we should desire him. He was despised and rejected by men; a man of sorrows, and acquainted with grief; and as one from whom men hide their faces he was despised, and we esteemed him not.

> C. Revealing truth! We confess before God and men that we have denied our Lord because we have been afraid of the reaction of men and we have been ashamed to own up to One crucified for us.

P. Surely he has borne our griefs and carried our sorrows; yet we esteemed him stricken, smitten by God, and afflicted. But he was wounded for our transgressions, he was bruised for our iniquities; upon him was the chastisement that made us whole, and with his stripes we are healed.

C. Amazing grace! We confess before God and men that Jesus Christ has borne our griefs and carried our sorrows; that he was wounded for our transgressions, yet by his stripes we have been healed!

P. All we like sheep have gone astray; we have turned everyone to his own way; and the Lord has laid on him the iniquity of us all. Yet, it was the will of the Lord to bruise him; he has put him to grief; when he makes himself an offering for sin, he shall see his offspring, he shall prolong his days; the will of the Lord shall prosper in his hand.

C. Joyous news! We confess before God and men that in the atoning death and victorious resurrection of Jesus Christ we are a forgiven people: a people set free to become all that God intended us to be. Praise be to you, O Christ!

The Lesson: Mark 14:53-72

The Hymn: Amazing Grace

The Drama and Meditation

The Offering of Our Gifts

The Distribution of the Card-of-the-Week

The Prayers

The Hymn:

The Benediction

(Copy for Card-of-the-Week)

MY PRAYER FOR FORGIVENESS

Lord, my God, I confess and lament before you that I am still too prone to sin and too little inclined to obey. Especially do I confess *(mention those things that need forgiveness)*. Merciful God, grant me again your forgiveness through the atoning death of my Savior. Set me free from all guilt and failure, all wrong and remorse, so that I may live for you and serve you. Amen.

Readings: Mark 14:53-72 and Isaiah 53

Use the back of this card to write the sin that has the tightest grip on your life and for which you seek Christ's forgiveness.

Feel Good Because God Has Forgiven You

CHARACTERS:
LOUISE
BOB
CHUCK
BETTY

LOUISE: Hello, how are you?

BOB: Fine! Just fine!

LOUISE: Hello! How are *you*?

CHUCK: Fine! Just fine!

LOUISE: Hello, how are you?

BETTY: Fine! Just fine! How are you?

LOUISE: Fine! Just fine! Couldn't be better!

CHUCK: Hello, there! How are you?

BOB: Fine! Just fine! How are all of you?

CHUCK, LOUISE, BETTY: Fine! Just fine!

LOUISE: Who are we kidding?

CHUCK: What do you mean?

LOUISE: Do you really care how I am? Aren't you scared to death that I might tell you?

BOB: You aren't supposed to say how you are. It's just a greeting people use.

BETTY: No one really cares how the other person is! . . .

CHUCK: Whether that person is sad, lonely, sick, discouraged, happy, on top of the world—or what!

LOUISE: That's right. If people answered that question honestly, the whole communication system of the world would break down!

BOB: You're expected to answer cheerfully and smile brightly and say, "Fine, just fine!"

BETTY: Even though you may be half-dying, bored, frustrated, or frightened!

CHUCK: Or thrilled and excited over some wonderful thing that has happened to you.

BOB: What would we say if we answered that greeting honestly?

LOUISE: Let's try again. Hello! How are you?

BOB: Fine! Just fine!—No, I don't mean that. I'm terribly unhappy.

LOUISE: If you want to tell me about it, I have time to listen.

BOB: No, I don't think I'm ready to talk about it yet, but thanks.

LOUISE: Hello! How are you?

CHUCK: You really want to hear? You don't just want me to smile brightly and say "Fine! Just fine!"?

LOUISE: No, I really want to hear.

CHUCK: Okay, then. I *am* fine. Just fine. I'm very happy today. I love God. God loves me. I love life. I love my fellow man. I love my job. I'm happy at home. Of course, *yesterday* things didn't look so bright! But I've been praying about things, and today—well, today things look just great!

BETTY: You haven't asked me to tell the truth about *me*. I'm angry—very angry, and disturbed. And *I've* been praying and I'm *still* angry and disturbed.

BOB: I just don't like myself at all today. And if I'm going to be honest, I don't much like any of you, or the world.

LOUISE: I understand how you feel. Often when we're hurting inside we don't like other people.

CHUCK: That's right. We feel about other people the way we feel about ourselves. Jesus said, "Love your neighbor as *yourself*." Most of our neighbors would be pretty miserable if we treated them the way we treat ourselves—hating and condemning ourselves, feeling guilty and self-destructive. We have to love ourselves first, before we can love our neighbor.

BOB: Doesn't that sound conceited—self-love?

LOUISE: What does love mean?

CHUCK: Understanding.

BETTY: Gentleness.

CHUCK: Patience.

LOUISE: Kindness.

BOB: Forgiveness.

BETTY: Appreciation.

CHUCK: Liking.

LOUISE: Having good feelings about someone even when we know their faults.

BOB: Encouraging and helping the other person to succeed—wanting him to succeed.

BETTY: Giving him approval even if he doesn't take the advice we want him to take!

CHUCK: Wanting the very best for that person.

LOUISE: So what is so terrible about applying all of those things to ourselves?

BOB: But I know myself. I know how awful I am, how ugly, distorted, judging, condemning and just—yechhhhhh!

BETTY: That's just the way I see myself too!

CHUCK: A friend of mine came up to me yesterday and said, "I know something terrible about you." I said, "Okay, tell me and let me add it to the list of all the terrible things I know about myself already!"

BETTY: I think that ties in with something I've been

struggling with. There's a man in this church I just can't stand. I think he's a phony, a big blabber-mouth and a liar. He's undependable, and irritable, and—I just don't like him! What's he doing in the church? And then I hate myself for feeling that way, and ask, what am *I* doing in the church!

LOUISE: Don't you suppose God can see all the same things about that person that you can see?

BETTY: You know it! I'm sure of it. He can't cover up those things from God!

LOUISE: And what if this person sees the same things about himself that you can see?

BETTY: Well, if he can, why doesn't he change?

BOB: Sometimes we can't change. By ourselves.

LOUISE: And don't you suppose God can see even more than you can?

BETTY: Yes, I guess so.

LOUISE: God can look into his heart and see how this man feels about himself. This man may not like the very things about himself that you don't like. He probably goes home at night tired and discouraged, hating himself.

BETTY: I hope so, but I don't believe it! He's too conceited.

LOUISE: Perhaps God sees good things about this man that we can't see. God can see how he is *going* to be, in the future.

BOB: We don't know the problems this man has. God knows them.

LOUISE: Have you thought where this person would be and what he would be doing if he weren't in the church?

CHUCK: Let's assume this poor man is doing the best he can . . . trying anyway . . . for none of us seems to succeed in doing the best we can . . . well, maybe it *is* the best we can do but we *want* to do better. Anyway, this poor man is struggling along —but what if he gave up, left the church, threw his faith away, even the little that he may have— would you want that to happen?

BETTY: I never thought of it that way. The church *is* the best place for him! God can reveal his sins to him, the same way he reveals my sins to me! You know, I can hardly wait to see this man and give him a big smile and handshake. I feel like congratulating him for getting along as well as he does!

LOUISE: Here's a thought. Maybe someone is looking at you and feeling the same way about *you* as you've been feeling about this other person!

BOB: Jesus said, "With the judgment you use in judging, so will you be judged in the same way" . . . sort of putting it in my own words.

BETTY: Now I feel guilty. What do I do with my guilt?

CHUCK: Jesus took our guilt upon himself. I thank him for going to the cross, and providing me forgiveness through his death before I was even *born!*

LOUISE: When I think of Christ on the cross—when I

think what his purpose was—a way of salvation for all who believe in him as their savior from sin—then I just can't feel sad. I want to shout with joy and say, "Thank you, Jesus, for dying for me . . . for all of us."

BOB: I agree. How can we moan, "Oh, what a shame that Christ had to die on the cross" when we know it was God's way of salvation for the world!

CHUCK: His sacrifice becomes our sacrifice. His death becomes our death. His victory over death, our victory, his righteousness our righteousness.

LOUISE: It's great to have a place to bring our problems, doubts, guilts, and sins.

BETTY: And to have a Savior from those sins.

LOUISE: If we confess our sins to Christ, he is faithful and just to forgive us our sins and to cleanse us from all unrighteousness. . . . Hello, there! How are you?

BOB: I'm much better now. Thank you for caring. How are you?

LOUISE: I'm fine. I really am just fine!

BOB: I've forgotten my unhappiness. I have so much to be happy about. I will forget myself and think of others.

CHUCK: The thing I was angry about—well, I'm still disturbed but I'm no longer angry.

BETTY: I got rid of my problem. My problem became a privilege. I feel loving toward the man I couldn't stand before.

Louise: Remember, Christ is saying to each one of us, "Hello! How are you?" And he really cares how we are. Christ said, "Behold I stand at the door and knock. If anyone hears my voice and opens the door, I will come in."

(Actors move down into congregation shaking hands with people as they say, "Hello, how are you?")

Feel Good Because God Has Forgiven You

Mark 14:53-72

How are you? Really? Suppose we would divide the congregation into small groups, in two's and four's, and ask you to honestly share how you really are. How do you feel about yourself? About other people? About the church? About God? We may find ourselves listening to some positive and happy insights. On the other hand, we would also be listening to all kinds of disappointments, feelings of failure, self-hatred, and bitterness. Just because we are Christians does not mean that automatically we feel good.

What if we asked Peter: "How are you, Peter?" What do you think he would reply? His reply would depend on *when* we asked him. If we asked Peter early on that first Maundy Thursday, we would receive one kind of reply. If we asked Peter early on the following morning, we would receive a radically different answer. And if we could ask Peter: "How are you?" a week or so later, the reply would take a hundred and eighty degree turn. Let us ask

Peter how he really feels at these three different times, listening not only to how Peter feels at the moment, but listening to how the Gospel of the forgiveness of sins deals powerfully with Peter's real problem.

Place yourself in the upper room on that first Maundy Thursday evening. The disciples have not yet entered. You have a few moments alone with Peter who with John helped prepare the Passover meal for Jesus and the other disciples. Ask him! "Peter, how do you really feel this evening?" In his answer Peter would reveal a heart filled with many questions about all that had been happening the last few days: the entry into Jerusalem, Jesus' teaching in the Temple, the great words of warning about last things, the parables that demanded watchfulness and faithfulness. Even in preparing for the Passover, a meal of celebration and joy, Peter felt an ominous cloud casting dark shadows on the festivities of that evening. Peter felt perturbed and unsettled about what was happening. But he felt quite sure about himself. His love for the Master he never questioned. His loyalty he never doubted. His faithfulness to the cause of the kingdom never gave reason for suspicion. "Peter, how are you really?" would have revealed such feelings before the Last Supper began.

Now place yourself on that Good Friday morning. Jerusalem is almost empty. People have gone outside the city wall to view a crucifixion of three condemned men. There you find Peter huddled by himself. You ask him, "Peter, how do you really feel today?" I believe you would be greeted first by silence. Then tears. Slowly, very slowly, you would hear words from a broken and agonized heart, words that reveal the hell Peter was going through. He would relate how he denied his Master before a maid and a bystander. How he hated himself! Peter wished that he had never been born. How he would have given his right arm—yes his left arm, legs, and eyes— just to have another chance, to be able to set the clock back twenty-four hours. What Peter would have given to have the opportunity to undo the horrible damage that he had done to his friend and Master, and to himself. For Peter nothing, absolutely nothing, would be able to undo the damage and the hurt and make all things new again.

Now place yourself by a lake a week or so later. It is early in the morning, and a fire is slowly burning itself out on the shore. A group of men are sitting around listening to another who by his very presence dominates the scene. After they disperse, you approach Peter and ask him the same question, "Peter, tell me, how do you feel today?" Peter would again have tears. But this time tears of joy! With a smile from ear to ear he would relate what had happened to him by the fire eating breakfast with the Master. Yes, with the Master! He whom they crucified, God raised up! As great as this miracle was, it is not what Peter shares with you. What makes Peter feel so completely happy in that moment is that the risen Christ of God had forgiven Peter. Suddenly Peter began to realize that his Lord's dying on the cross was for him, on behalf of him, taking Peter's sins with him.

Peter now knew what it was to be a sinner. And Peter also discovered what it was to be forgiven. Peter realized that not only men in general needed forgiveness, not only the mass of people needed an atoning Savior, but that he, Peter, needed Jesus most of all. Everything became real for him because he became so personal. Peter woke up to the power of the forgiveness of sins. Forgiveness made his life new and exciting again. It canceled out the shame and the guilt. It freed him up and offered fresh possibilities for loving his Master. It let him feel good about himself, all because of the crucified and risen Lord Jesus.

Are you ready to share from the heart how you really feel? If you are burdened with any sin, any guilt, any hate, you should feel free to share it with a brother or sister. Don't let it fester inside your heart where it will poison your whole body and soul. Expose it in the cleansing light of God's forgiveness. Your brother and sister in Christ are not here just to listen, but to speak to you the words of forgiveness in the power of the risen Christ. As we speak the word of Christ's forgiveness to each other, we will feel the strength and the joy tht makes life new and exciting again.

So how are you really? Before you answer, see the risen Christ standing next to you. Feel his arm around you. Listen to his words of forgiveness and promise. Now, how are you, really? Jesus makes all the difference in the world. With Jesus you can feel good because God has forgiven you.

5

Face Life with Courage

Order of Worship

The Prelude

The Hymn:

The Responsive Reading

    P. St. Paul said, "For the word of the cross is folly to those who are perishing, but to us who are being saved it is the power of God (1 Cor. 1:18). For I am not ashamed of the gospel; it is the power of God for salvation to everyone who has faith (Rom. 1:16).

    C. Lord, give me the courage never to be ashamed of your saving gospel.

    P. St. Peter said, "For to this you have been called, because Christ also suffered for you, leaving you an example, that you should follow in his steps. He committed no sin; no guile was found on his lips. When he was reviled he did not revile in return; when he suffered, he did not threaten, but he trusted in him who judges justly" (1 Peter 2:21-23).

C. Lord, give me the courage and the faith to follow in your steps.

P. St. John wrote, "Do not fear what you are about to suffer. Behold, the devil is about to throw some of you into prison, that you may be tested, and for ten days you will have tribulation. Be faithful unto death, and I will give you the crown of life" (Rev. 2:10).

C. Lord, give me the courage not to back away from making the right decisions, but in everything to remain faithful to you—the way, the truth, the life.

P. Jesus said, "If any man would come after me, let him deny himself, and take up his cross and follow me. . . . For whoever loses his life for my sake will find it. For what will it profit a man, if he gains the whole world and forfeits his life?" (Matt. 16:24-26).

C. Lord, give me the courage to lose my life for your sake, no matter what the cost, so that I may receive the full and abundant life now and forever.
Praise be to you, O Christ!

The Lesson: Mark 15:1-15

The Hymn:

The Drama and Meditation

The Offering of Our Gifts

The Distribution of the Card-of-the-Week

The Prayers

The Hymn:

The Benediction

(Copy for Card-of-the-Week)

MY PRAYER FOR COURAGE

Lord, my God, some decisions are difficult to make, especially when they involve doing and saying the right thing for the sake of Jesus Christ. I think of a special decision I would like to make for his sake this week —————. Give me the courage and the faith to make that decision to your glory. Amen.

Readings: Mark 15:1-15; Matthew 16:24-28; 1 Peter 2:18-25

Write down the decision you want to make and pray over it.

Face Life with Courage

CHARACTERS:
Don
Joan
Mark
Lorraine

Joan: What does it mean to live with courage?

Mark: Courage is the opposite of being *dis*couraged!

Lorraine: Courage is carrying on when you're discouraged—until Christ changes discouragement into courage.

Don: When we live with courage we get rid of all discouragement! Simple!

Joan: I think of someone very brave going into the lions' den. That's courage.

Mark: Or of David meeting Goliath.

LORRAINE: I think living with courage is having the strength to get up every morning!

DON: That's right. We put courage opposite some big, frightening task, when it may be just as courageous to keep on doing the small, daily tasks.

JOAN: The Bible says, "This is the way; walk in it." To me, courage is the continuing walk, no matter how feeble our steps are.

MARK: I continually need Christ-centered-courage ... or I'd never make it through the day. That's three c's.

LORRAINE: Nights are the worst time for me ... waking up in the darkness ... feeling all alone and discouraged.

DON: Why don't we act out what courage is?

JOAN: *That* will take courage!

MARK: Only we won't pretend! We'll use situations in our lives when we really need courage.

LORRAINE: How do I get rid of my mother-in-law? She's the most discouraged person I know. She is always afraid ... afraid she'll get sick ... afraid I'll get sick ... afraid the children will get sick ... afraid of having no money ... afraid, afraid, afraid. Everything is too hard or too much trouble for her. Yet she talks about trusting God and goes to church every day and twice on Sunday!

DON: Act it out! Pretend you're talking to her on the phone.

LORRAINE: *I* don't do much talking.

DON: Well, this time *you* do the talking!

LORRAINE: Well, all right . . . *(pantomimes holding phone)* . . . Hello . . . un huh. un huh . . . oh, that's too bad! I'm sorry to hear that . . . un huh. No, I'm not tired. No, I'm not sick! . . . Hey, stop! Listen to me! Stop being so negative and discouraged. Stop being so depressed and depressing. Stop dwelling on all the negative fears and morbid possibilities. You say you have faith in God, so have faith! Put your faith into practice. Start having joy in your life. I'm not tired and I'm not sick, but by the time you finish with me, I *feel* tired and sick! I need encouragement and you need encouragement, so let's encourage one another. I'll see you next week. Good bye.

DON: How do you feel?

JOAN: Just great! I wish I had the courage to talk to her that way. I'm always afraid I'll hurt her feelings so I let her hurt mine and ruin my life. Well, I *will* tell her the next time she calls!

DON: You have the courage. Put it into practice.

LORRAINE: How would you like to put *your* courage into action?

DON: I'd like to talk to my boss. He's always telling off-color jokes . . . and swearing. I get so tired of it but I've been afraid to say anything.

LORRAINE: So talk to your boss! Next time it happens, let him know how you feel.

DON: A practice session in courage! All right . . . I'll say . . . Mr. Jenkins, I want you to know that I am offended by your jokes and stories. To me they are crude distortions of love and sex. I can't laugh at such things. I think these jokes are examples of bad taste.

I've never said anything about your swearing because I thought I would lose my job. But Mr. Jenkins, it hurts me to hear you use the name of Jesus as a swear word.

I just had to let you know how I feel about this, Mr. Jenkins, because you are not the kind of person who would deliberately offend anyone. Thanks for letting me get this off my chest. Now I'll get busy and do the best job I possibly can for you.

JOAN: That's the idea. Now it's your turn, Lorraine.

LORRAINE: I get depressed and discouraged and it's not the way I want to be. I'll practice on myself! ...Look, you! I'm sick and tired of the way you go dragging around looking at the sad part of life all the time. Start living what you listen to in church! ... IIow am I doing?

JOAN: Just great. Keep it up!

LORRAINE: Stop looking at yourself all the time and look to Christ. Walk with him. Appreciate each day. There may not be too many of them left. So enjoy what God has given you today. Be cheerful. It doesn't cost anymore than being pessimistic all the time... Look up at the sky and thank God for the sunset. Thank him for every good thing in your life ... Hey! I like this. I'm going to try it more often. Your turn!

MARK: I need courage at work. I sell out in many different ways. I don't want to express an opinion for fear I might be disagreeing with someone else. I live in fear. I compromise God in my life.

Don: Do you want to talk to yourself?

Mark: No.

Joan: Do you want to talk to your boss?

Mark: No.

Lorraine: Do you want to talk to someone you work with?

Mark: No.

Don: Then who do you want to talk to?

Mark: I want to talk to God.

Joan: Practice *praying?*

Mark: That's the weak place in my life. I don't pray enough and ask God for courage. Well, here goes! *(looks up, eyes open)....* God, I'd like to talk to you. I'm afraid all the time. I forget that you have promised to be with me. You know my problems and fears. Help me to remember that your power and glory surround me. I'm your child. Help me to lift my head high and have courage, constant courage in all the small things of the every day— and for the important moments when I need to have the courage to stand up and be counted. I want to be counted, God, on your side! Give me Paul's courage: whether I live or die, I belong to you. My real job is getting you first in my life. We're partners ... Thank you, God.

Don: It works, doesn't it?

Mark: It really does.

JOAN: I need to practice courage at night. I wake up and begin going over all the problems in my life. Fears come out of the woodwork and gnaw at me. I think of what I have to do and I think of what I've failed to do as I lie there staring in the darkness. I get stiff with fear and frustration. There's a sour taste in my mouth. My stomach cramps. When I do manage to get some sleep, I can hardly wake up in the morning! Then, in the morning, I'm too tired to do anything about what I was worrying about the night before!

MARK: So what do you want to practice?

JOAN: During the day I commit everything to God, and then at night I take it all back again! I'm going to turn everything over to God *all* the time. Then I'll have the strength to do the job he wants me to do during the day. If I wake up during the night I'll lie there and praise God! That's better than wasting time worrying.

DON: We can have Christ-centered-courage-constantly. That's *four* c's!

JOAN: Christ-centered-courage-constantly. I like that.

LORRAINE: The Christ-courage to do the everyday thing that has to be done with peace and joy and love.

MARK: Remembering that Christ had the greatest courage of all, courage enough to die.

DON: And he tells us, "Let not your hearts be troubled or afraid. I will be with you until the end of the world."

JOAN: Let's stop sitting in a spiritual stew all the time and walk with the Lord.

LORRAINE: When we have a complaint, we'll ask Christ what he wants us to do about it.

MARK: We'll change our complaints into commissions for Christ.

DON: When we have a problem, we will focus on the solution. We will change our divine discontent into dedicated deeds!

LORRAINE: Hey! That's four d's. Divine discontent into dedicated deeds.

MARK: We'll thank Christ for the courage He gives us to carry out those Christ-commissions and dedicated deeds.

JOAN: Remember, we can have practice sessions in courage anytime we need them and God will be there to help us when we practice and when we're going through the real thing. "I can do all things through Christ who strengthens me."

DON: It's thrilling to see where God can guide us in our thinking.

LORRAINE: Discouragement will change to discovery with Christ.

MARK: Life with Christ is the great adventure!

ALL: Amen!

Face Life with Courage

Mark 15:1-15

In the drama we heard one of the actors say, "Practice courage. A good idea! Now it's your turn." We may like the first part that urges us to practice courage because it is a good idea. But we hesitate, if not pull back altogether when we hear, "Now it's your turn." Like the parachutist standing by the open door of the plane, you sense fear when the instructor says, "Okay, now it's your turn." You suddenly realize that you must jump. You no longer can talk about it or look at others do it. You must do it.

In many areas of our life we feel we have no courage. We know what we should do. But we do not have the mettle to do it. It would be unwise for anyone to belittle another because of the lack of courage. The decisions that call for courage often have far-reaching consequences. If you stand up to your boss and tell him how you feel about his swearing and off-color jokes, he can make things hard for you at work. You wonder if standing up to him is really worth it all. If you feel you must, you wonder what would be the best way.

More often having courage is in the area of smaller things. You feel you lack the spirit to share what you really feel with your spouse, or you lack the tenacity to be consistent in the discipline of your children. When we lack courage in doing what we feel must be done, we begin to look down on ourselves. We feel that we cannot always face ourselves honestly, much less others.

Therefore, when we hear that with the power of God as revealed in Jesus we can face life with courage, we wonder how it is possible. Yet we believe that the Gospel of Jesus Christ is really the power of God that transforms people from being timid and afraid into people who are confident and strong. Another way of saying it is that the Gospel can give each of us a stronger faith, for faith and courage are closely related. Nothing gives a person more courage to face life with a bold spirit than a lively faith in the word and promises of God.

Pontius Pilate did not have courage because he did not have faith in God. We have thought to ourselves, "If only Pilate would have had the courage to stand up for what was right and just, to administer justice in the tradition of Roman law and fairness, his name would not have been associated with those who compromise principles. He would have been numbered with the saints of God."

We may have said to ourselves, "If I had been in Pilate's place, I would have stood with Jesus no matter what." But Pilate did not stand with Jesus. It was not that Pilate had no conscience. Pilate had some real fears. And fear drives out courage, even as fear can drive out love. He feared a revolt by the mob, and not without justification. The leaders knew this fear. Pilate's position, yes his very life, was at stake at this time with the powers in Rome. So courage gave way to expediency. To cover up his act of injustice he passes the buck to the crowd. By this act Pilate becomes one of the most pitiable characters in the history of our planet. The meeting with his God on that fateful Good Friday instead of being his salvation, became his condemnation.

Isn't that the way it is with us many times? We pass the buck. We do the convenient thing, the safe thing. God meets us in a situation, and instead of standing with him, we turn the other way. We think first of ourselves, our families, our position, our investments, and let these important commitments override the issue of right and wrong, truth and false witness, good and bad. That is why many end up like Pilate, washing their hands of the issue. To face life with courage is more than an enviable virtue. It is the way to live victoriously and confidently no matter what. It is the way to live honestly with ourselves, knowing that there is more to life than those things that threaten us.

This way is what the Gospel wants to give us. To stand with Jesus is to know that there is more to life than anything that may threaten us. With Jesus we don't have to run or pass the buck. Jesus did not pass the buck. He didn't run. He was not afraid to rock the boat, even if it cost him his life. He did not go back on the word of his heavenly Father. He did not give up on the world, not even on Pilate, because he knew that his Father did not give up on the world. Jesus did not wash his "lily-white" hands in the safety of the heavens and refuse to get them dirty with the evil of men. Jesus knew the cost of his decision. That is why he pleaded, "Father, take this cup from me." Yet Jesus did not run or pass the buck. Jesus had courage.

Jesus had courage because he put his complete trust in the heavenly Father. Jesus did not give way to his fears, but could face the cross because he put himself completely into the will and the word of his heavenly Father. "Father, into your hands I commend my spirit," were his last words. They were words of complete trust and courage.

What does this all have to do with courage? Everything! We do not have courage by talking about it or by whistling in the dark. To practice courage is to practice our faith. To practice our faith means we take God at his word and live by it no matter what. That word assures us that God cares for us, that he will always be dependable, that he gives us the abundant life, and when we fail out of fear, he is there to forgive us and lift us up. Paul put it this way, "If God is for us, who is against us? . . . in all these things we are more than conquerors through him who loved us!"

Courage, then, is bound up with what we believe. What we believe gives us our convictions, and our convictions help us to act with courage. You believe in Jesus. Jesus is God's way of giving you victorious living. With him you can face your life with new courage.

6

Live Life with Love

Order of Worship

The Prelude

The Hymn:

The Responsive Reading

P. When we were still helpless, Christ died for the wicked, at the time that God chose. It is a difficult thing for someone to die for a righteous person. It may be that someone might dare to die for a good person. But God has shown how much he loves us: it was while we were still sinners that Christ died for us!

C. Lord, our God, we confess our amazement at how much you have loved sinners like us.

P. The love of Christ controls us, because we are convinced that one has died for all; therefore all have died. And he died for all, that those who live might live no longer for themselves but for him who for their sake died and was raised.

C. Lord, our God, let this love of our Savior control our minds and our bodies, so that with our minds and bodies we might live in his invincible love.

P. Dear friends! Let us love one another, for love comes from God. Whoever loves is a child of God and knows God. Whoever does not love does not know God, because God is love. This is how God showed his love for us: he sent his only Son into the world that we might have life through him.

C. Lord, our God, help us to love one another as you have loved us.

P. This is what love is: it is not that we have loved God, but that he loved us and sent his Son to be the means by which our sins are forgiven. Dear friends, if this is how God loved us, then we should love one another. No one has ever seen God; if we love one another, God lives in us and his love is made perfect within us.

C. Lord, our God, live in us and perfect within us your love. Praise be to you, O Christ!

The Lesson: Mark 15:21-39

The Hymn:

The Drama and Meditation

The Offering of Our Gifts

The Distribution of the Card-of-the-Week

The Prayers

The Hymn:

The Benediction

(Copy for Card-of-the-Week)

MY PRAYER FOR LOVE

Lord Jesus Christ, I need to be caught up more and more in your love. Fill me with your love so that I can love others as you love them, and love myself as you love me. By the power of your cross, move me into your way of loving people. At this hour, I want especially to have this love for ————— ——————————————. Thank you, Lord. Amen.

Readings for the Week: 1 Corinthians 13; Mark 15:21-39

Use the back of this card to write down the names of those whom you especially want to love with the love of Jesus Christ.

Live Life with Love

CHARACTERS:

Paul

Jerry

Mary

Kay

Paul: Live with love!

Jerry: What is love?

Mary: God is love.

Kay: So it's important that we try to understand what love is so we can better understand God.

Paul: The Bible says there is no greater love than to give up your life for your friends.

Mary: So how do we give our lives for our friends— and enemies?

JERRY: Love is forgetting yourself and remembering others.

KAY: Love is putting yourself in the other person's place so that you understand his needs.

PAUL: Love is putting the other person in your place, putting his needs ahead of your own.

JERRY: My being up here and taking this part is love! I didn't want to, but you needed me so here I am!

KAY: Love is sacrificing our own desires for the good of others.

JERRY: Just think about that for awhile! That sounds like a cliche until you put it into practice! Sacrificing *our own desires* for the good of the other person! That *is* love. And it really hits me where it hurts.

PAUL: The fact that people came to church is an act of love—to God and to each other.

MARY: Just think, right now, all kinds of people are doing all kinds of things at this very moment as acts of love.

JERRY: Doctors, nurses, fathers, mothers caring for sick children . . .

KAY: Fathers and mothers working to support their families . . .

PAUL: Children obeying their parents . . .

MARY: People obeying God's commandments.

JERRY: What commandments has God given us about love?

KAY: Love little children.

PAUL: Love widows and orphans.

MARY: Love the poor, the sick, the dying.

JERRY: Love the lonely.

KAY: Love your *enemies*.

JERRY: That's the tough one! I can say it but I can't do it!

MARY: Love purity . . .

PAUL: Love good . . .

MARY: Beauty . . .

JERRY: Honesty . . .

KAY: Even as Christ loved us so we are to love all others.

PAUL: He gave us the example of his love.

MARY: He points the way and gives us his power.

JERRY: To love ourselves . . .

KAY: And love our neighbors as we love ourselves . . .

PAUL: And to love God.

JERRY: Well, I think all this talk about love is stupid and I think we're stupid for mouthing such platitudes. We're just going around in circles.

PAUL: When we swallow the angry words that leap into our mouths and give a soft, loving answer instead, that is love . . . *I* have just loved *you* for I swallowed my angry words.

MARY: We are to love those who persecute us.

JERRY: Oh, how can I? This is all very lofty talk but how can I love someone who is telling lies about me, someone who is ruining my life?

KAY: He can't ruin your life unless you let him. If your heart is filled with hate for him, you will ruin your own life. If you fill your heart with God's love, you will love him.

JERRY: All right, I'll try. But it's a lot easier to *say* the words than it is to *live* them! . . . "Love them that persecute you. Have sympathy for those who would spitefully use you! ". . . Demonstrate love to me.

MARY: A love demonstration! A great idea.

PAUL: All right. What if someone right over there hates you. What will you do to demonstrate love for him?

MARY: *(Swallows hard.)* I will think loving thoughts, and send them in his direction. "I do not hate you. I'm trying to love you. I feel sorry for you. I'm sorry that you are filled with hate for me. It's harder on you than on me." Then I will smile at him . . . and if he sneers at me—I will keep right on smiling! I hope it works. At least, I'll *try!*

PAUL: What will you do if someone hurts your feelings?

KAY: I will try to remember that they are not my feelings. My feelings are dead. As Paul said, "I die daily to the old self and walk in newness of life in Christ." We are to be dead to self, and alive in Christ.

JERRY: What will you do if you are thinking mean thoughts about someone else? That's what I'm doing right now!

PAUL: I will ask the Holy Spirit to cleanse me and take all bitterness out of my heart and fill me with the fresh, clean water of love.

JERRY: All right, here's one! How would you show love to *Satan?*

PAUL: *(Thinks a moment.)* I would—point him to Christ on the cross. There is no greater love than that.

JERRY: And if Satan comes to tempt you, what love will you show him then?

PAUL: I will show him Christ's love that covers me.

MARY: Would you destroy your enemies? Love them. Change your enemies into friends!

KAY: Would you conquer mighty armies? Love them!

PAUL: Love is feeling, doing, giving, serving.

MARY: When we change our impatience into patience, that is love.

MARY: It's love when we change our jealousy into trust.

PAUL: To be in a hurry, and stop and do something for someone else ...

JERRY: To be annoyed at a motorist, and instead of honking or shaking a fist, or shouting something, you smile ... *that's* love!

MARY: To want something very much, and then when you get it, give it to someone who wants it more than you do, that's love.

PAUL: To see a wrong that needs righting, and to pitch in and right the wrong, even if you may get into trouble, that's love.

KAY: Love is guidance . . .

JERRY: Correction . . .

MARY: Discipline.

PAUL: Denial.

KAY: We ignore the one great commandment God has given us, "Love one another," and we feverishly try to do everything else under the sun.

JERRY: Make money.

MARY: Create artistic masterpieces.

JERRY: Become famous.

PAUL: Study and learn great knowledge and wisdom.

KAY: Be popular. Use the right toothpaste.

JERRY: Collect possessions and comforts.

MARY: But the most important thing God wants us to do is to love one another.

PAUL: Love is patient . . .

KAY: Gentle . . .

JERRY: Kind . . .

MARY: Longsuffering . . .

PAUL: Quiet . . .

KAY: Fair . . .

JERRY: Honest . . .

MARY: Strong . . .

PAUL: Eternal.

KAY: Love can slip through any barrier . . . any defense . . . love cannot be shut out.

MARY: To put love into an everyday situation. My daughter left her two cats with me when she moved away. It could be an annoyance to have to feed and water them. But I am filled with love as I do it, love for the cats and even more for my absent daughter. She can't see me as I take care of them, but I do it as an expression of my love for her.

KAY: I have habits that annoy my husband. When I correct these habits, I'm doing it as an expression of my love for him.

JERRY: I have habits that annoy my family. When I correct them, I'm showing them that I love them.

PAUL: Christ said that if we love him we will keep his commandments, so we express our love to him everytime we obey God.

MARY: When we talk about love demonstrations, the greatest love demonstration of all time was a cross . . .

JERRY: . . . at Calvary.

KAY: Before we were born, God loved us.

PAUL: While we were yet in our sins, Christ loved us.

MARY: Though indifferent to him, with our backs turned to him, he loved us and prepared a place for us.

JERRY: Yes, the greatest love demonstration of all time. "God so loved the world that he gave his only son that whoever believes in him shall not perish but have everlasting life.

KAY: The crucifixion was love in action.

PAUL: Let us go, in the spirit and strength of Christ and the Holy Spirit, to be a demonstration of God's continuing love.

MARY: We'll be so consumed with demonstrating God's love that we won't have time for anything else.

PAUL: With the cross of Christ continually before us, let's seek ways to demonstrate Christ's love to everyone we meet.

JERRY: Right now, in your hearts, have a love demonstration in your feelings and thoughts, right where you are sitting.

PAUL: Is there someone you hate? Ask God to change that hate to love.

KAY: Are you breaking God's commandments? With God's help determine to keep the commandments as an expression of love to God.

MARY: Have you wronged someone? Ask God to help you make it right. Do you need to say you're sorry to someone? Do it right away.

JERRY: Let's all be love demonstrations wherever we go . . .

MARY: Whatever we do . . .

PAUL: Think love . . .

KAY: Act love.

JERRY: God gave his love to us, let us receive that love.

MARY: The greatest love demonstration we can make is to accept God's love gift to us by receiving Christ as our Savior, our Redeemer, our Lord . . .

KAY: And sharing that love with everyone we meet.

PAUL: God goes with you. Go in love.

Live Life with Love

Mark 15:21-39

"Be a love demonstration wherever you go," was one of the concluding lines in our chancel drama. You may think to yourself, "We try, but it doesn't work." Think again! The Holy Spirit created the church to be a genuine "love demonstration" in the world. Pagan observers of the early church exclaimed, "Behold, how they love each other!" Whenever and wherever the church is alive in the Spirit of God it is a "love demonstration."

For example, you cannot talk about the wonderful vocation of healing and medicine in our world without talking about the influence of the Christian church. Wherever the church has gone with the Gospel of God's love in Christ, it has always reached out to heal the broken and diseased bodies of people.

You come back and say, "That may be true. But so often the church has been a demonstration of prejudice, lovelessness, and even hatred." With heads bent low we must admit that the church has not always been a "demonstration of love."

The problem is that people, including Christians, refuse to receive God's gift of love that he has given us in his Son. Mark's dramatic telling of the crucifixion highlights human response to God's love. God sends his Son into the world, and we crucify him. By nailing him to the cross we reveal how unbelieving and sinful we are. All of our talk about love suddenly becomes cold and meaningless. "This is love. Not that we loved God, but that he loved us and sent his Son to be the expiation of our sins," writes John (1 John 4:10). So God's kind of love places our kind of love under judgment. God's love is as different from our ordinary kind of loving as the fourth dimension is from our third dimensional world. No matter how many slogans we make about love, how many bumper stickers shout the merits of love, or how many songs sing out, "All we need is love," it still does not change people into loving others with God's kind of love.

That is the problem. If we could live life with ordinary love, we would not need Jesus. God would not have had to demonstrate his kind of love by sending his Son. But God sent his Son so that we could live life with his kind of love. God's love is unconditional; ours is conditional. His love is pure; ours is not. God's love is eternal; ours is temporal; God's love is self-motivated; ours is object-motivated. God's love is self-giving; ours, too often, is self-satisfying. To live in God's love is like living in another dimension.

The Good News is that you can live life with God's dimension of love. And as the cross and open tomb demonstrate most clearly, this love is powerful. It not only shatters hatred and lies and lust, but it changes people to love others in a new and exciting way. When you begin to love others with God's dimension of love, you become different, and so often the other person becomes different, too. God's love is a power that works. With this power the early church turned the world upside down. Now that's a "love demonstration" for you.

To see how this can work in your life and mine, let us look at a young seventh grader by the name of Debbie. Debbie was in confirmation class when she inadvertently blurted out that she hated another girl at school. The class had just been studying the words of John's first letter, "Any one who hates his brother is a murderer, and you know that no murderer has eternal life abiding in him" (1 John 3:15).

The pastor asked, "Debbie, how can you have eternal life and still be filled with hate?" "I don't know," she replied, "but I still hate her!" The pastor then asked the class to counsel her in this problem. "Look at the girl's good points," was one suggestion. "She has none," was the reply. "Just try harder, Debbie, then you can love her a little bit," was another's advice. "I have tried, but I only hate her more."

After a few minutes, the pastor said, "Debbie, the problem is that you are operating on merely a human level. You are trying only with your kind of love, and that is proving inadequate. You need to reach up to a love resource outside of yourself. This week for your homework pray several times each day for Jesus to fill you with his dimension of love. Only Jesus has the kind of love to change your thinking."

The following week the whole class was waiting for Debbie's report. The pastor asked, "Well, Debbie, did you do your homework? What happened?" Quietly Debbie responded, "Yes, I did. I prayed for Jesus to fill me with his love, so that I could love her with his love. And do you know what happened? Yesterday she came up to me and said, 'Can we be friends?' I think that God's love works. I don't hate her anymore."

God's kind of love does work. It worked the miracle of our redemption in the atoning death of his Son. And it continues to work that miracle in the life of any person who believes it.

Do you have trouble in loving someone? Do you find that your heart harbors all kinds of prejudices and hatreds against people? Then draw on the heavenly dimension of God's love which he has poured out in Jesus. Try it. Discover again how much God really loves you and what this love has done for you. Then let this love become the dynamic in loving others. You will be surprised what it does to you, first of all. And you will be surprised how it can change others. The Gospel is bound up in this kind of love. That is what it is all about.

Believe it: with Jesus you can live a life with love!

7

Live a Joyful Life

CHARACTERS:

Lloyd

Bernice

Brian

Christine

(Costumes should be bright colors for Easter. Flowers and bright colored drapes may be used for a setting.)

LLOYD: Christ is risen!

ALL: He is risen indeed!

BRIAN: Welcome to Easter!

BERNICE: There is music!

CHRISTINE: And flowers!

LLOYD: Happiness . . .

BRIAN: And joy!

LLOYD: Welcome to this Easter morning!

BERNICE: Wait a minute! Why should we welcome EASTER morning?

BRIAN: Easter means Christ is risen!

BERNICE: No, it doesn't. Easter was a pagan festival long before Christ was ever born!

CHRISTINE: I didn't know that.

LLOYD: True. Easter was a pagan day recognizing spring and fertility, death of winter, birth of spring.

BRIAN: Then that's where we get the Easter bunny and Easter eggs, and the custom of wearing new spring clothes!

CHRISTINE: I've always wondered where we got such a conglomeration of chocolate bunnies and the crucifixion, rites of spring and the resurrection of Christ!

BRIAN: So what brought the Christian festival of Easter and the pagan festival of fertility together on this day?

LLOYD: The early church decided that since the resurrection of Christ occurred *about* the same time as Easter, and since Easter was already celebrated as a special festival of the pagan peoples, it would be an easy substitution for the new converts to the Christian faith to worship Christ in the midst of the Easter festival!

BRIAN: I should think that would mean confusion.

LLOYD: It did. That's why there is so much confusion today.

BERNICE: The same thing happened to Christmas.

CHRISTINE: What do you mean?

BRIAN: Don't tell me that *Christmas* is pagan!

BERNICE: No, not Christmas. Christmas means the mass celebrating the birth of Christ.

LLOYD: But Christ wasn't born on December 25th. He was probably born months before. The date of *December 25th* was a pagan celebration centuries before the birth of Christ.

BRIAN: So that's where we get the Druid rites, the Yule log, mistletoe and holly, the elves and merry-making!

CHRISTINE: Yes. December 25th was the celebration of the days getting longer again. The short days of winter were over.

LLOYD: So the early church decided to celebrate the birth of Christ on this pagan holiday—

BERNICE: To make it easier for the Christian converts to worship Christ on their familiar pagan holiday.

BRIAN: I always thought the pagan rites were crowding in on our spiritual days!

CHRISTINE: No, just the other way around. The church was trying to cut through pagan customs with the new Christian celebrations.

LLOYD: That's what happened to Sunday as well. Sunday was a pagan festival to worship the sun . . . sun day. More than five centuries after Christ died, Constantine moved the Sabbath from Saturday to Sunday to make it easier for the pagan converts to worship God on their familiar sun worship day

BRIAN: Now lots of things are becoming clear to me.

BERNICE: That's what happens every day in the Christian life. The new life of Christ cuts across all the customs of the old life, the sin, the sorrow—and gives us victory in Christ.

CHRISTINE: So whether the day is called Easter—

BRIAN: Or Christmas—

LLOYD: Or Sunday—

BERNICE: Or Monday—

LLOYD: Or Tuesday—

BERNICE: Or any day of the year—

BRIAN: Our response is the same.

ALL: Christ is risen! He is risen indeed!

LLOYD: That's why Easter is joyous.

BERNICE: That's why *every* day is joyous, not just Easter.

CHRISTINE: We don't have to wait for Easter to celebrate the resurrection of Christ. Easter is every day.

BRIAN: But I don't feel anything special today. I'm tired. I'm not feeling as strong as I used to feel. My job is difficult. I'm feeling discouraged, I guess. Just plain old down in the dumps.

LLOYD: No matter what our personal feelings are—they cannot change the glorious fact of our new life in Christ.

BERNICE: Our response is the same.

ALL: Christ is risen! He is risen indeed!

CHRISTINE: The one I love doesn't love me. There have been angry words, unkindness, misunderstanding. We have quarrelled and it is hard to forgive. I am not filled with love today.

BRIAN: Love never fails. God loves us. In the same way that God loves us, we should love one another. God loves us even when we don't deserve it.

LLOYD: We should love others though they may not deserve it, even as we hope they will love us even though *we* don't deserve it. God is love no matter how we feel.

BERNICE: Our response is the same.

ALL: Christ is risen! He is risen indeed!

BERNICE: My heart is full of grief today. My child is dead. Last week I stood at the edge of the open grave. It is too soon for joy. The sharp pain of loss is filling my heart.

BRIAN: Christ knew about weeping. He wept for Lazarus. He wept for Jerusalem. He wept in the garden.

CHRISTINE: Mary wept for Jesus by the open tomb.

LLOYD: God knows about sorrow and weeping and grieving.

CHRISTINE: His hand shall wipe away all tears.

LLOYD: He will change your grief into glory. Trust him. Commit your grief to him.

BRIAN: Christ gives us victory over death. In the midst of death is everlasting life.

BERNICE: Our response is the same.

ALL: Christ is risen! He is risen indeed!

LLOYD: But I have doubts. I have no faith. In place of a shining eternity for me, there is only gray, swirling emptiness. Instead of being held in the hand of God, I am plunging down into nothingness! I have no proof there is a God.

CHRISTINE: Christ is that proof. He lived and died and rose again in ringing triumph that shouts, "There is a God! He is our Heavenly Father!"

BRIAN: Faith is the gift of God.

BERNICE: Accept that gift. Receive it and say, "Thank you, God."

LLOYD: Everyone has doubts. We are all doubting Thomases at one time or another in our lives.

CHRISTINE: Christ said to Thomas, "Thomas, you have seen me and have believed. Blessed are they *who have not seen me* but have believed."

BRIAN: Whatever our doubts, our fears this day—

BERNICE: Our response is the same.

ALL: Christ is risen! He is risen indeed!

LLOYD: Make that your greeting to all this day!

CHRISTINE: Shout it out from the mountain top!

BERNICE: Whisper it at the edge of the grave.

CHRISTINE: Murmur it as you give a kiss of love.

LLOYD: No matter where you are!

BRIAN: Or what time it is!

LLOYD: Or who you are with!

BRIAN: Or what the conditions are!

BERNICE: Our response is the same!

ALL: Christ is risen! He is risen indeed!

LLOYD: Amen.

Live a Joyful Life

Mark 16:1-8

Prayer: Victorious Lord, by your mercy free us from all powers that would rob us of the full joy to live fully in the knowledge of your resurrection. Amen.

Begin by speaking the traditional Easter greeting with the congregation. Say, "Christ is risen!" Have them respond, "Christ is risen indeed!" Repeat until everyone is saying it loudly and clearly.

Yes, we have to say it. Out loud. With conviction and joy. We have to say it so that others around us can hear the glad news. It cannot be held in. It must be shouted from the housetops. CHRIST IS RISEN! We need to speak the glad news. And we need to hear the glad news. Again and again. Like the "I love you" spoken between husband and wife, it never grows stale. It always becomes new. But we have to say it.

Nothing in heaven or earth is more exciting than the resurrection of Jesus Christ. The resurrection gives life to everything the Scriptures talk about. The resurrection makes everything new and meaningful for the Christian. That is why it is exciting. And shouldn't it be for everyone? The message of Easter produces faith and fresh joy for real living. And that is what we want to think about this happy Easter day—WITH THE RISEN CHRIST YOU CAN LIVE A JOYFUL LIFE.

Yet we do not always feel our hearts beating with a new pulse, nor do we feel our blood throbbing with a happy surge. Too often we feel like somebody old, not new. Even on Easter this is the way some of us feel. We still yearn to experience the fulness of being reborn and becoming what God has intended us to be.

Often we are like the women who hear the Easter message from an angel's lips, yet flee in fear, saying nothing to anybody. Here was the day of days, and they go on living as if nothing happened. Yet it is really not so strange. For we, too, go about in our daily lives as if it hadn't happened. We go out into life, too, filled with our fears . . . saying nothing to anyone.

The Easter message too is often swallowed up by our fears. We feel the world with its pressures pressing harder against us than the words of the angelic messenger: the demands at work, the bills that relentlessly crowd our mails, the traffic that jams the freeways, the schedules that hold us fast to places and times, the god mammon that makes its own rules and values. Little wonder why we are afraid, for the world with its pressures would bury us. Yet deep inside, we know that life is more than "what we put on" or "what we eat." We hear the still, small voice saying quietly, "Man does not live by bread alone."

Some of us are afraid, not just because of the burdens we have to carry, nor because of the guilt that haunts us from deeds past done. We are afraid because God seems so very far away in all of this. Some of us feel what has been termed "a cosmic loneliness." We see ourselves very much alone with our anxieties and cares, our guilt and remorse. Even God seems very far away, too far to really care or help. The other morning at the early hour of 3 A.M. the phone woke me up. On the other end a young person, gripped with this nightmare of cosmic loneliness wanted to talk. Talk with someone. For God was too far away.

Some of us know all too well the fear that comes because of death. We are afraid of death and dying. We remember dear ones who have died and have become holy memories. Death can be a shroud that engulfs us even on Easter morning, that keeps away the genuine joy of the sons and daughters of God. Let us not be surprised at this discovery that we have fear, for all these fears are very real.

Yet at the very moment the women in our text were filled with fear and bewilderment, the truth still stood that Jesus was not in the tomb, for God had raised him up! The women's fears and the disciples' unbelief did not cancel out the reality of Christ's victorious resurrection. In the days that would follow the truth of the resurrected one would catch up to them and overwhelm them, but on that first Easter morn the text plainly states that they were filled with fears. Yet Christ was risen! And that the text states plainly, too!

Some of us still remember the wild joy that followed the news of victory in World War II. But that wonderful news did not reach all the towns of Norway, which for so many years had experienced the harsh reality of Nazi occupation. So for many days, even weeks, many citizens of Norway lived as subjected people under the heel of the German army. They were in fact free, but did not know it. They lived in their fears with no hope.

What a parable of so many of us! We live as if Jesus Christ the Son of the living God has not been raised up from the dead. We live in our unbelief, refusing to let the promises of God's word be true for us. We live in our fears that cancel out genuine joy for living. We need Easter, to speak and hear the message until we feel our hearts beating with a new pulse and our blood throbbing with a happy surge.

The angel announces: "Do not be amazed; you seek Jesus of Nazareth, who was crucified. He has risen, He is not here; see the place where they laid him."

The Apostle Paul exclaims: "But in fact Christ has been raised from the dead, the first fruits of them who have fallen asleep" (1 Cor. 15:20).

The Apostle Peter proclaims: "This Jesus . . . whom you crucified . . . God raised up!" (Acts 2:23-24).

Now this is news, indeed, but what makes this *good* news is that it is for *you.* Angels and apostles are all excited about this news because Jesus Christ has been raised up from the dead. What God did on Easter in his Son, God did for you, because he knows your fears and the reality of your human situation. You want to see what you will become? Take a good look at the resurrected Lord.

So what shall we say to all this? Do we still want

to leave this morning with our fears and say nothing to anyone? Do we still want to be like the doubting disciples and say "unbelievable"? Do we want to go home and say nothing to anybody? Do our fears still loom as pressing and over-powering?

Or, does not the Easter news of the risen One excite us with a new joy for living?

Leave this morning determined to say something about the risen Christ to someone. Start with your family, around the table, with the relatives coming over for Easter dinner. Read the Gospel again! Sing an Easter hymn! Put a banner on the wall that says, "Christ Is Risen!" Or as one little girl painted on a large, round stone, "Smile! He Lives!" But please, don't be silent. You need to say it. Others need to hear it.

But most of all you need to believe it. Believe it with all your heart. It is for *you*. Not just for mankind in general. But for *you*. See yourself today in the light of the open tomb as somebody new ... somebody given a new birth ... somebody with possibilities of becoming more than you dreamed. And feel new, see new, think new, react new, love new, live new. You can. Because the victorious One says to you, "I am the resurrection and the life," and you can find yourself saying, "You really are!"

And taste what is still to come. What a destiny! What a future! What a life! Live with joy!